Numerology

How to Embrace the
Synchronicities of Angel Numbers

*(Discover How Numerological Divination is
Connected to Astrology Tarot and Ayurveda)*

Tony Lucia

Published By **Phil Dawson**

Tony Lucia

Numerology: How to Embrace the Synchronicities of Angel Numbers (Discover How Numerological Divination is Connected to Astrology Tarot and Ayurveda)

ISBN 978-1-998769-81-0

Legal & Disclaimer

The information contained in this ebook is not designed to replace or take the place of any form of medicine or professional medical advice. The information in this ebook has been provided for educational & entertainment purposes only.

The information contained in this book has been compiled from sources deemed reliable, and it is accurate to the best of the Author's knowledge; however, the Author cannot guarantee its accuracy and validity and cannot be held liable for any errors or omissions. Changes are periodically made to this book. You must consult your doctor or get professional medical advice before using any of the suggested remedies, techniques, or information in this book.

Table Of Contents

Introduction

Have you ever thought about why you have been blessed with certain traits and faculties? Have you ever felt lost for periods of time? Do you want to know what your options are for the future?

In my personal life I was at the point of being very confused. I didn't know what was going on, why certain events were happening in my life and why I felt so overwhelmed, or why I felt out of my control. I certainly didn't know what I could do to get out of the hole I had created for myself. When I learned about Numerology I felt like I had finally discovered an answer to all my questions.

When I first started it was a bit difficult, however, after spending time researching various types of Numerology, as well as its benefits and drawbacks, as well as the many ways Numerology can shed light on the problems I was facing I realized it was something I needed to tell everyone I could.

This book will teach you how you can do exactly what I, along with millions of others, have accomplished to improve our lives.

Numerology can unlock the secrets for you, and reveal how you can be your most authentic self.

The following chapters will explore the history behind Numerology and the meaning and energy behind the numbers. We will discuss the metaphysical characteristics that numbers possess, the advantages of personal Numerology, and the connections to Numerology such as crystals, Astrology, Tarot, and music. We will also discuss the different types of Numerology as well as the meaning of the planets as well as the signs of the Zodiac.

We will learn how to read your natal chart and use it, as well as the Pythagorean Arrows, to determine your life path, soul drive and karmic cycles. We will end with a discussion of Life Path compatibilities, Essence Numbers and the mysteries of Reincarnation.

Using Numerology will give you the ability to determine the true nature of your personality and personal obstacles to living as you reach your full potential in your life. You will gain valuable information about your relationships and discover the type of relationship you would be a good fit in. You will be able to discover information about yourself that will help you find your purpose in life.

Numerology will show you how to set your own goals, as well as how to understand past failures, and how to take action that will benefit you and allow you to develop your full potential.

Chapter 1: The Science Of Finding Your True Potential And Your Life Mission

Numerology: A History

Numerology, in simple terms, refers to the investigation of numbers and their meaning and impact on our daily lives. People who believe in numerology believe it is a method that is mathematically accurate in determining one's future, as well as personality luck numbers, past lives, and much more, based on the significant numbers in one's daily life.

This practice known as Numerology has been practiced since the dawn of mathematics and in the 6th century the Pythagoreans are believed to have been among the first to advocate the idea that numbers have meaning in the spiritual realm rather than just representing mathematical concepts. It is not uncommon for cultures and peoples to assign a specific meaning to numbers or a specific significance Seven is believed to be lucky for many people, while thirteen is often associated with bad luck. This concept goes back millennia. Numerology simply takes that idea and takes it one step further.

When practicing Numerology, regardless of the type-which we will examine in the next chapter-it is essential to be aware that numbers are metaphysical. They are associated with the alphabet, the planets, the chakras and the Tarot, as well as with crystals and music, and also with colors and colors. That is why so much can be learned from the study of the personal birth chart.

There are three main varieties that make up Numerology, Pythagorean (or Western), Chaldean and Kabbalistic, however New Kabbalistic, Chinese and Abracadabra Numerology are also used. In the next chapter, we will review each of these in detail, the history behind them, their application, and so on. For now, it is only important to make sure that regardless of which form of Numerology you choose to work with, it is important to adhere to the specific form. The differences between the different types could lead to more confusion when you are trying to master more than one, especially when you are just starting out.

Investigating the metaphysical nature of numbers and their vibrations.

The most important numbers that Numerology examines include 1 through 9 and The Master Numbers 11,,, and 22. Three numbers that are significant as they suggest more strengths and difficulties. Each number has its own unique vibrations and energy that can be harmonious - or not, depending on circumstances such as music, crystal colors, chakras, lifestyle choices, etc.

Vibrations are discussed in depth in Chapter 6, which will be devoted to the birth date number. Simply put, each number is unique and has its own particular vibration, similar to that of each color, gemstone or crystal, etc.

Numerologists believe that numbers are metaphysical. The metaphysical concept is that abstract concepts such as cause, known being, substance and space are a philosophical branch that has its roots in reality. Because Numerology can be used to discover the vast amount of information available, it is natural that numbers are considered metaphysical as they offer insight into these abstract subjects.

The Benefits of Personal Numerology

Numerology provides a wealth of benefits that can be incorporated into your daily life. Numerology is a great way to understand the nature of your personality, compatibility and life-changing events, as well as preferences, and much more.

Personal Particularities

Numerology is a great way to identify or gain insight into your personal characteristics, usually through the use of something called a Personality Number. We'll look at this in more detail in Chapter 7, but for now it's enough to understand that the Personality Number is one of the most fundamental numbers (i.e. Life Path Number or Expression Number Birth Day Number, etc.) and reveals how other people initially perceive you, along with the traits they expect to see.

Compatibility and Interests

Chapter 9 is devoted to compatibility with your partner, but this is not the only type of compatibility where numerology can help you. Compatibility with specific jobs and organizations can allow people to avoid unhappiness or wasting time in a career or job that will not be fulfilling in the long run because it is not compatible with their. The Birth Number is often used to determine this. Your fundamental numbers, especially your Life Path Number, will allow you to determine what types of activities you are likely to enjoy or excel in.

Life Changes

Numerology can reveal circumstances and events that are likely to occur within your life based on your personal numerology. Using this information can be helpful in preparing for those major (or minor) life occasions, giving you a greater chance of success or positive outcomes in the process. The same goes for decreasing the chances of something happening.

Using your Life Power and Path numbers throughout taking your 3 life cycles and personal years, pinnacles as well as transit energy and obstacles into consideration so you can make more informed and better decisions about the choices you make within your life that will lead to these major or minor changes. As the saying goes, he who is forewarned is always forearmed.

Numerological Associations Colors

We talked about vibrations in the previous section, and there are colors that align on a vibrational level with certain numbers. Each number from 1 to 9 has primary and secondary colors that activate or potentiate the vibrations and characteristics of the number. This list is available below.

Primary: red

Secondary: apricot, crimson

Primary Orange

Secondary: salmon, gold, black

Primary: yellow

Secondary: amber, ruby

Primary: green

Secondary: brown, blue, blue, silver, indigo

Primary: blue

Secondary: cherry, pink

Primary: indigo

Secondary: orange, mustard

Primary: violet

Secondary: magenta, pearl

Primary: pink

Secondary: ivory, opal

Primary: gold

Secondary: red, olive

There are also certain personality characteristics for one's primary color:

Red: risk-taker, dominant personality, visionary, passionate, energetic, courageous, flamboyant, tenacious.

Orange is loyal and content and is easy to be with, mentally and physically well balanced

Yellow: cheerful, intelligent and self-confident. He is charming, creative, a great negotiator and leader, mysterious.

Green: down to earth, logical in reality, unselfish, committed, difficult to influence

Blue: optimistic, empathic and idealistic, patient, loving, flexible and maternal.

Indigo: sensitive, inquisitive, inquisitive, curious old soul Indigo: impulsive, ambitious and curious

Violet: affectionate and cerebral old soul, affectionate and wise romantic, artistic

Rose "Pink": love, strength and leadership

Gold: compassion, joy, understanding, and love.

If you have ever felt attracted to a particular hue on a particular day, it usually means that the qualities you are looking for are either not present in you or at the present time, or you want to enhance them. Therefore, you should be aware of your feelings and dress accordingly because the energy and vibrations can positively influence your day and allow you to achieve goals that you might not otherwise be able to.

Crystal Numerology Associations

Crystals are powerful instruments that contain their own energy, just like every living thing on Earth. Certain crystals, as well as certain colors, are compatible with the frequencies of specific numbers, including the number of the path of life. Since crystals possess physical, emotional and mental abilities to help heal and provide energy, blending them with the life path number can produce powerful results.

We will discuss ways to identify your personal life path number in a later chapter. We will just list some gemstones and crystals that are associated with numbers 1 through 9.

Garnet, aquamarine, obsidian, turquoise, sapphire.

Smoky quartz, rutilated quartz tourmaline, tanzanite

Amazonite, amber, amethyst, amethyst, diamond, pyrite, blue topaz

Jade, bloodstone, emerald, moonstone, black sapphire, clear quartz

Aquamarine, heliodorite, alexandrite, zincite, carnelian

Bloodstone peridot Jasper, citrine onyx, marble cat's eye, peridot

Fluorite, pearl, labradorite, rose quartz, agate

Citrine, cinnabar, ivory, opal, jet, selenite, smoky quartz

Feldspathic malachite and sandstone Yellow topaz pink and brown tourmaline Hematite, rose quartz

Numerology Tarot Associations

Tarot or tarot readings is a divinatory technique performed with an average deck of 78 cards. 56 of them are called "the minor arcana", while the remaining 22 are called "the major arcana". There are an infinite number of decks to choose from. The most popular is the so-called Ryder-Wait Tarot. These readings are done to identify possibilities of outcomes, as well as to assess the impact of influences affecting people, events, or both simultaneously depending on the question asked of the cards. They are not designed to "tell the future" in the conventional sense. However, they can be used to help make decisions when the path seems uncertain.

The Minor Arcana

The Minor Arcana The Minor Arcana are used to understand the physical world. They are classified into four categories called suits: Wands, Swords, Cups and Pentacles. Wands represent willpower, Swords are associated with the mind, Cups correspond to emotion and Pentacles are related to material things or the physical world. The cards of these suits are numbered from 1 to 10 and contain an element linked to them which is Earth, Air, Fire or Water. Wands are linked to Fire, Swords to Air, Cups to Water and Pentacles to Earth.

The four suits, which are linked with their correspondences, can be used to gain knowledge and insights on specific topics. Knowing how the cards work in relation to the numbers can be a fantastic method for gaining a wealth of knowledge about oneself.

The Major Arcana

They represent important life events and are considered archetypal. This implies that, not only do they have a greater significance than the suits, but they also have spiritual significance. The 22 cards are numbered similarly to the suit cards, however, they are from 0 to 21. If one views the cards as if they were an illustrated storybook, and reads the cards in order one will see the story of a child's life from infancy (The Fool) to the point of enlightenment (The World).

The importance of numbers in the Tarot

Because both the Major and Minor Arcana are numbered, it is crucial to think about the meaning of the card as well as the number, since five cards correspond to the numbers 1 through 10. While all 5 cards are numbers 4 or 4, the meanings can differ greatly depending on the specific card, but it is common that the message behind is the same in all cards.

For example, the number 1 is related to the Ace of Pentacles, Ace of Cups, Ace of Swords, Ace of Wands and the Magician. Each of these cards has different meanings, but in all of them the theme of "new beginnings" is cross-cutting. It is useful to know that when reading the Tarot each number is considered cyclical. Odd numbers suggest fluctuation and change, while even numbers suggest stability.

Below you can find an alphabetical list of the numbers 1 through 10, as well as their meanings/associations with the Tarot cards and their meaning with the numbers.

The only card with the zero includes the Fool.

This card is a symbol of innocence and the beginning of everything.

The cards associated with the number one are: the Magician Ace of Cups, also known as the Ace of Cups, the Ace of Spades, the Ace of Pentacles and the Ace of Wands.

Magician: The deck represents the power of manifestation, as well as actions.

Ace of Cups card: Symbolizes the creative thinking of love, creativity and new relationships.

Ace of Swords: This card symbolizes mental clarity, success and fresh concepts.

Ace of Pentacles The Ace of Pentacles is a symbol of the possibility of a new career path (career-wise, as well as financially) prosperity, abundance and manifestation.

Ace of Wands: This card is a symbol of new opportunities, potential and the ability to inspire.

The cards bearing the number 2 are the High Priestess and the Two of Cups, the Two of Swords, the Two of Pentacles and the Two of Wands.

The High Priestess card symbolizes sacred wisdom, intuition and the divine feminine.

The Two of Cups card symbolizes relationships, mutual attraction and unifying love.

The Two of Swords: The card symbolizes the need for avoidance, making difficult decisions and weighing various options.

The Two of Pentacles symbolizes time management, flexibility and many priorities.

The Two of Clubs card symbolizes the future, decisions and the process of discovery.

Cards that are associated with the number 3 include the Empress Three of Cups, the Three of Cups, the Three of Swords, the Three of Pentacles and the Three of Wands.

The Empress card: A symbol of beauty and abundance, the feminine and the natural world.

The Three of Cups: This card symbolizes collaboration, friendship, celebration and creative thinking.

The Three of Swords. This card symbolizes the emotions of grief, emotional pain, sadness and sorrow.

The Three of Swords deck symbolizes collaboration, teamwork and execution.

Three of Wands: This card is a symbol of expanding progress, growth and the ability to see forward.

The cards that are associated with the number 4 are the Emperor, the Four of Cups, the Four of Swords, the Four of Pentacles and the Four of Wands.

The Emperor card symbolizes authority, establishment and structure.

The Four of Cups symbolizes reflection, re-evaluation and meditation.

Four of Swords The Four of Swords card symbolizes relaxation, meditation and rest.

The Four of Pentacles card symbolizes control, security and conservatism.

The Four of Clubs: The card is a symbol of homecoming, joy and celebration.

Cards that are associated with the numbers 5 include the Hierophant The Hierophant, the Five of Cups, the Five of Swords, the Five of Pentacles and the Five of Clubs.

The Hierophant card is a symbol of spiritual wisdom, tradition and conformity.

Five of Cups: Symbolizes regret, sadness and pessimism.

Five of Swords: The card symbolizes conflict, disagreement and even defeat.

Five of Pentacles: The symbolizes poverty, financial loss and loneliness.

Five of Clubs (also known as the Five of Wands): This deck represents differences, diversity and tension.

Cards bearing the number 6 include the Lover of Cups, the Six of Cups, the Six of Swords, the Six of Pentacles and the Six of Wands.

The Lover: It is a card that represents harmony in relationships, choices and love.

The Six of Cups card is a symbol of nostalgia for childhood, love and innocence.

The Seven of Swords: This card symbolizes changes, transitions, an act of passage.

The Six of Pentacles symbolizes generosity, giving as well as sharing money.

Seven of Clubs: The card symbolizes public recognition, self-confidence and the possibility of success.

The cards that are associated with the 7 are the Seven of Seven, the Seven of Cups, the Seven of Swords, the Seven of Pentacles and the Seven of Wands.

The Chariot: It is a symbol of determination, willpower and control.

The Seven of Cups is a symbol of possibilities, choices and illusion.

Seven of Swords This card is a symbol of deception and betrayal.

The Seven of Pentacles deck symbolizes lasting results, investment and endurance.

Seven of Wands This card symbolizes the concept of challenge, competition and also protection.

Cards that are associated with the number 8 include Strength and the Eight of Cups, the Eight of Swords, the Eight of Pentacles and the Eight of Clubs.

It is a card of strength that is a symbol of influence, strength, as well as persuasion.

The Eight of Cups card symbolizes loss and displeasure.

The Eight of Swords card symbolizes negativity and victimization.

8 of Pentacles: The symbol symbolizes mastery, repetitive tasks and skill development.

The Eight of Clubs card symbolizes alignment, action and the ability to move.

Cards that are associated with the numbers 9 include the Hermit Nine of Cups, The Nine of Cups, the Nine of Swords and the Nine of Pentacles, and the Nine of Wands.

The Hermit The Hermit: This card symbolizes the soul's search for introspection, soul searching and inner guidance.

The Nine of Cups: Symbolizes gratitude and happiness.

Nine of Swords The Nine of Swords card symbolizes depression, anxiety and worry. anxiety. anxiety.

Nine of Pentacles: The deck symbolizes financial freedom, as well as luxury and wealth.

Nine of Clubs: The symbolizes limits, courage, as well as the ability to overcome.

The cards that correspond to the number 10 are the Wheel of Fortune, the Ten of Cups, the Ten of Swords, the Ten of Pentacles and the Ten of Wands.

The Wheel of Fortune: This card symbolizes destiny, karma and the cycles of life.

The Ten of Cups: This card is a symbol of divine love, harmony and alignment.

Ten of Swords: This card is a symbol of an unsettling ending, loss or crisis.

Ten of Pentacles: The is a symbol of contributing financial security, and wealth.

10 of Clubs: The card symbolizes the completion of a task, burden, and hard work.

The remaining four cards that are not numbered include Pages, Knights, Queens as well as Kings in each of the suits. These Major Arcana cards, 11 through 21, can be reduced to single digit numbers as they have a similar meaning and simplify things.

Numerology and Music Connections

You may not be sure how music and numbers work together, however they do. Many famous composers you have encountered have mixed music and numbers.

Some of Plato's manuscripts are even believed to contain mathematical symbolism for musico-mathematical use. Plato accomplished this by dividing an octave into twelve tones. After dividing his entire text into 12 it was discovered that there were "positive concepts" that were associated with the intervals of the Pythagorean scale, which were harmonious, as well as dissonant intervals that contained negative concepts.

You may be thinking why this was so important and the answer is quite simple. Plato thought that the whole world was controlled by numbers and not by the gods, which prompted him to initiate Pythagorean Numerology. In the period of Plato's life and according to the Greeks his work was to be classified as scientific, musical arcana. This was important as it implied that additional meaning could be discovered in his writings if one was able to decipher their meaning.

Famous composers such as Schumann, Bach, Schoenberg, Peter Maxwell Davies, Berg and many other musicians have incorporated numbers into their music. Many even used mysterious numbers to convey their deeper musical meaning.

Numerological Organizations Planets in Astrology

Astrology is the idea that one can learn information by studying the movements of the planets and their positions, specifically those that occurred at the time and date you were born (if they are related to you, then obviously). In simple terms, Astrology is the study of the movement of the planets and their orbits, however, as with Numerology there are numerous aspects to this method.

The Sun influences identity and life. The Moon influences security and emotions, Mercury influences communication and the mind, Venus influences relationships and desire. Mars influences action and motivation, Jupiter influences abundance and luck, Saturn influences limitations and lessons. Uranus influences change and rebellion, Neptune influences imagination and optimism, and Pluto influences transformation and power.

Your Zodiac sign is the one that determines your primary traits, also called your Sun sign, however this does not mean that it is the only Zodiac sign you will find in your Astrology chart. We are all an amalgamation of various Zodiacs, and planets residing in different Houses, which has a different influence on us.

The most popular numbers in Astrology are 1 through 9. There are nine planets that are part of our solar system, each of which corresponds to one or more of the numbers. People born on specific dates are ruled by certain zodiacs and planets. The 9 digits will ring a bell, as they are the fundamental numbers also used in Numerology.

One of the most important

The Sun

Birthday of any month: 28 19 10 and 1

Ruler of the Leo planets

Two

The Moon

Birthday of any month: 29 20 11 and 2.

The planetary ruler of Cancer

Three.

Jupiter

Birthday of any month: 30 21 12 and 3.

The Planetary Ruler of Sagittarius and Pisces

Number four

Uranus

Birthdays of any month: 31, 22 13, and 4.

Five.

Mercury

Birthdays of any month: 23, 14, and 5.

The planetary ruler of Virgo and Gemini.

Sixth number

Venus

Birthdays of any month: 24 6, 15 and 24

The Planetary Ruler of Libra and Taurus

Seventh number

Neptune

Birthdays of any month: 25 or 16, and 7.

Planetary ruler of Cancer

Number eight

Saturn

Birthdays of any month: 26, 17, and 8.

The planetary ruler of Aquarius, Capricorn and Libra

Number nine

Mars

Birthdays of any month: 27, 18 and 9

The Planetary Ruler of Scorpio and Aires

Both Astrology and Numerology are intrinsically related, as many calculations are used to read your astrological chart, plus numbers are present in almost every aspect of our lives.

Numerology Chakra Associations

The human body has seven Chakras that contain the spiritual energy that flows through the body. The 7 Chakras are located at the top of the head, around the neck and along the spine. From the highest to the lowest, they comprise from top to bottom: the Crown Chakra, the Third Eye Chakra, the Throat Chakra and Heart Chakra, the Solar Plexus Chakra as well as the Sacral Chakra along with the Root Chakra.

Each Chakra is identified by the Numerology number associated with it, and provides more information about the Chakra as a whole, and what it is for and when combined with other Chakras.

1. Root Chakra

Traditional Names: Mooladhar

Color Red

Major Arcana Cards The Emperor The Emperor, the Devil and the World

Planet Saturn

Zodiacs: Aquarius and Capricorn

Two: Naval Chakra

Traditional Names: Swadhisthana

Color The color is orange.

Major Arcana Cards The Empress, the High Priestess and the High Priestess

Planet: Jupiter

Zodiacs: Puzzle Pieces and Sagittarius

Three: Solar Plexus Chakra

Traditional name is Manipura

Color: yellow

Major Arcana Cards The Chariot the Tower the Sun

Planet: Mars

Zodiacs: Aries and Scorpio

Four Heart Chakra

Traditional name Anahata

Color: Green

Major Arcana cards: The Lover, Justice, Strength, Temperance

Planet: Venus

Zodiacs: Taurus and Libra

Five Throat Chakras

Traditional name: Vishuddhi

Color Blue

Major Arcana Cards The Magician and the Hierophant and the Wheel of Fortune

Planet: Mercury

Zodiacs: Gemini and Virgo

Six Third Eye Chakra

Traditional name is Ajna

Color: indigo

Major Arcana Cards: The Moon The High Priestess, The Moon The Hermit

The Moon and the Sun The Moon and the Sun

Zodiacs: Cancer and Leo

Seven 7: Crown Chakra

Sahasrara is the traditional name.

Color Violet

Major Arcana Cards: The Hanged Man The Star and the Fool The Judgement

You may have noticed that the Crown Chakra (Sahasrara) does not have a planetary or Zodiac assignment. This is because the Chakra is believed to be the State of Divine Bliss, in which no other information is needed.

Chapter 2: The Universal Truth Of Numbers

In Chapter 1, there are many types of Numerology. In this chapter, we will look at the different forms, starting with the three main types.

Western or Pythagorean Numerology

This type of Numerology is the best known and most widely used. It was developed by the Greek metaphysician, astrologer, musician and mathematician Pythagoras, who lived in the 6th century. It is not clear if Pythagoras was the true creator of Numerology or if he was only one of the first to apply it and spread its teachings to his students. However, the fact remains that he used Numerology to predict future events and the fate of individuals who were divine and much more.

Pythagoras believed that each planet was associated with a particular sound and was represented by particular numbers. He believed that classifications such as introverted or extroverted man or woman beautiful, ugly, or ugly are elements from which it was possible to explain the numbers.

The method of making use of Pythagorean numerology consists of assigning nine fundamental numbers (1 to 9) to the Greek alphabet. The Pythagoreans consider that the numbers repeat themselves. When the number 10 is reached, 1 is multiplied by 0 to arrive at 1. This is the same for any number that is a composite (other than any of the master numbers) since they can all be reduced to a single digit number.

The meanings of the basic numbers of Pythagorean Numerology are explained below.

Creation

Omniscient

Creativity

Stability and resilience

Unpredictable, energetic, dynamic

Mothering, caring

Looking, thinking

Balance, power

Idealism which is the principle of life.

In the Pythagorean type of Numerology there are two types of frequencies that are basic and master. The numbers 1 through 9 contain basic vibrations, like any other two-digit number that can be reduced to a single-digit number. There are two numbers of master vibrations: 11, and 22, which do not combine to make a single digit number. These master numbers symbolize the Karma that determines someone's success or failure in their current situation. Both master and basic numbers are characterized by positive and negative aspects as everything in life.

In addition to the master numbers there are also karmic debt numbers - 19, 16, 14 and 13. In the words of Pythagoras and his followers, these numbers reflect the results of previous lives that were so bad that they created a karmic debt that carried over to the next. Karmic numbers are explored in greater depth in Chapter 7, when we examine the frequency their names carry. It is normal to use both the date of birth and your name to determine the meaning of Western Numerology, and as with Chaldean and Chaldean, which we will explore further in the chapter we discuss the links between these numbers.

As with the karmic debt number, each number has positively and negatively charged energy connected to it. This is vital to keep in mind as people often wonder if they are compatible with a partner, family member, friend or even colleagues. While analyzing the numbers it is crucial to keep both sides in mind. Even when two people's life numbers appear to be similar, there is a possibility that they may not match. This is due to the fact that one could be bringing negative energies into the numerology of the other. In order for this not to happen, it is necessary to understand the expectation one has of the partner.

Pythagorean Numerology uses aspects such as the soul impulse number, life path number, personal numbers, Pythagorean Arrows, names, expression numbers, as well as a maturity number, to decide the destiny of an individual. We will go over all of these factors in greater detail throughout this book, as well as instruct you on how to identify each of these numbers for yourself!

At this point all you have to keep in mind is the fact that the basis of Pythagorean Numerology begins with 6 fundamental numbers: three from your child's name and three from your birthday. These six numbers are called the six vibrations. They are the number that represents your life path The birthday number the number of the first impression the number of the inner soul or vowels, the number of the characters or consonants, as well as your numbers of expression.

Kabbalah Numerology

This is the type of Numerology that is commonly employed when reading names and is almost as well known as the Western Numerology of Pythagoras. Kabbalah Numerology originated with Hebrew mysticism. It was based on using the Hebrew alphabet and its 22 vibrations to aid in divining information. It was later modified into Greek, as well as the Roman alphabets, as well.

The 10 different energy sources used in Kabbalah calculations are Malkuth, Yesod, Hod, Netzach, Taphareth, Geburah, Chesed, Binah, Chokhmah and Kether.

The word originates from the 13th century Kabbalists, who believed that the Old

Testament was a secret code ordained by God and used Numerology to unravel it, hence the name Kabbalah Numerology. It is believed that Kabbalah also played an important role in occultism such as Tarot reading. Incredibly, there are 22 letters in the Hebrew alphabet, and there are 22 Major Arcana cards, and it is believed that they connect and offer a greater understanding of each other, because each of the 22 Major Arcana cards are specifically identified by numbers.

Other forms of Numerology such as Pythagorean and Chaldean, for example, you need to know not only your name, but also the date of birth, time of birth and so on. For Kabbalah Numerology all that is required is the person's name. It is naturally simpler, however, it leads some practitioners to believe that it is not entirely effective, as it does not provide the same depth of knowledge, since you are only extracting information from the person's name. There are some important details that the date of birth, time or other information. can reveal, and even without the additional numbers, we are not able to access the additional details.

Like Pythagorean Numerology, each letter of the alphabet is linked to a specific number. However, these numbers only help to determine an initial numerical value. Kabbalah has over 400 path numbers, which makes it difficult to identify the right Kabbalah number for a person if one decides to study all possible paths. Many prefer to concentrate on the numbers that are common to this reason.

To determine your Kabbalah number, you should

Translate the letters of your personal name (first, middle and last name are included) using the Hebrew translation alphabet.

1. A, J, S

2. B K T

3. C 3: C, L and U

4: D 4, M 4: D, M

5 5: W, E and W

6 6. F, O 6: F, O

7: G P, G, Y

8 Z: H, Q, Z

9 I 9, R

All numbers

Divide this total by 9

Add 1 to the result of the previous step: this number will be your personal Kabbalah number.

Let's look at an example. Let's say your name is added to 44. Then you can do the following:

44 / 9 = 4.8

8. The remainder.

8 + 1 = 9

The number 9 represents your Kabbalah number.

When you have a number equally divisible by 9, for example, 36, then you can simply view the number as 36.0 Add 1 to 0 and that will give you a Kabbalah number of 1.

Kabbalah numbers from 1 to 9, and the meanings they convey.

Development

Increase

Affection

Uselessness

Genesis

Implementation

Mysticism

Impulsiveness

Luck

While the different types that make up
Numerology translate their alphabets into
numerical numbers but do not translate in the
same way as well as the identical
alphabet/number match. In Pythagorean
Numerology, it is noted that including the 9

also disregards all information after the eight letters or numbers.

New Kabbalistic Numerology

This particular form that is part of Kabbalah Numerology was derived from the Roman alphabet interpretation. Like the original version used, this one is based on one's name instead of birthday and employs Pythagorean processes to calculate the dates. This is because the New Kabbalah Numerology focuses more on the life events of the individual's characteristics.

Luria developed a theosophical framework that, according to his followers, fostered an economic thought system of dialogue, thought and critique that, at the same time, offered a comprehensive description of humanity's role within the global community in a way that is morally, spiritually and intellectually important to us. This led to the creation of the New Kabbalah.

The goal of the New Kabbalah is to develop or enhance the philosophical and psychological meaning of symbols and ideas that are fundamentally Kabbalistic. Unlike many other types of Numerology that are used, the New Kabbalah uses a blend of Hinduism, Platonism, Buddhism, Gnosticism and Jewish mysticism, which allows this form to be more encompassing than conventional Kabbalah Numerology.

The location of its New Kabbalah number is identical to the original version, the only difference being that it is taken into account in conjunction by the psychological and philosophical practices mentioned above.

Chaldean Numerology

Chaldean Numerology, which is often called Mystical Numerology is closely connected with Astrology as it is derived from Mesopotamia The place that was the beginning for Western Astrology. This type of Numerology is also linked to the Kabbalah as well as the Indian Vedic system. It is believed to be a more accurate version than

Pythagorean Numerology. However, it is less well known due to its difficulty.

This type of Numerology uses a system that is difficult for many to understand or even master. The values assigned to the alphabet are not systematic as they are for Pythagorean Numerology as well as Kabbalah. Chaldean Numerology is often referred to as mystical numerology due to the fact that it focuses on the occult and metaphysical aspects of one's personality and destiny. In simple terms, this type of Numerology is used to discover forces invisible to the naked eye, which could influence a person's life.

The Chaldean people invented this type of Numerology and have contributed significantly to mathematics, Numerology, Astrology and many other fields of study due to their extensive study.

Chaldean Numerology is distinguished from other types of Numerology for a few different reasons. The first is that the name the person uses to guess is not necessarily the name he or she was born with or the name by which he or she is best known. Another distinction is that their number system is based on 1-8 rather than 1-9. This is because 9 is considered a sacred number. It is one of the highest sacred numbers today. The only case where the number 9 is used is when your name is a 9. This implies that the letters assigned to each number differ from the letters used for Kabbalah and Pythagorean Numerology.

According to the Chaldean Numerology System, the numbers are represented by the letters in the following order.

1 A, I, J Q 1: A, I, J, Q

2 2: B 2, K R

3. C 3, G 3, S

4. D 4, M and T

5. E 5: E, H, N 5, X

6. U, V, W

7. O, Z

8. F, P

Chaldean Numerology uses the person's date of birth and believes it is the second most significant aspect of its research. It also consists of adding up the numbers that make up the name of one's choice. The meaning of each number is exactly the same as in Pythagorean Numerology. However, in Chaldea more than one number of one digit is used. It is essential to know how to judge any compound number, as they are a symbol of the metaphysical and/or deeper meaning behind the name.

These numbers are obtained by adding three (or two if the person does not have a middle name) digits of each name, without reducing them to single numbers. Once you have the single digit and composite numbers, it is time to include the date of birth in the formula.

Suppose, for example, that the person for whom we are performing a Chaldean reading is Ann Marie Jones, and that she was born on June 2, 1984.

First, determine the formula for determining the names beginning with the letters "1, the middle name and the numbers of the last name.

First name First name: 1+5 + 5 = 11.

Middle name Middle name 2 , 1 + 5, equals 13.

Last name Last name: 1 + 7 + 5 + + + 3 = 21

Step 2: Reduce each number to one digit, but note the number of composite numbers to determine the name.

First name First name: 1 . + 1 equals 2.

Middle name 1 + 3 =

Last name Last name: 2 + 1 = 3

Step 3: Add the three together.

2 + 4 + 3= 9

Step 4: Determine your date of birth. For example, June 2, 1984, which is 06/02/1984.

0 + 6 + 0 + 2 + 1 + 9 + 8 + 4 = 30

Step 5: Reduce the number of digits to one.

3 + 0 = 3

Once you have all the necessary numbers and information, you can analyze their frequency. It is possible to determine the difference between your name and your full name has negative or positive vibrations. Single digit numbers indicate how others perceive your appearance. All numbers refer to aspects or influences that are not visible, that may play an important role in your life, that you may not be aware of, or in certain cases provide clues or predictions for the future.

It is essential to remember that each composite number has a distinct meaning based on its roots (1 from 1 to 9), as well as the numbers 10 to 52 have an even deeper and more specific meaning. Most people stick with 52 because it is the 52nd week of the year There is no need for most people to go any further.

Here is the correspondence of each number according to Chaldean Numerology.

Self-sufficient and dominant

Adaptability and compatibility

Creativity

Discipline

Freedom, travel

Active, enthusiastic

Curiosity

Ambition, determination

Helpful, compassionate

Greater possibility of achieving honor

Dangers of life

Anxiety and pain

Power and change

Financial and/or business luck

Favorable when paired with a positive value, otherwise unfavorable.

Be extremely cautious when making an important or big decision

Lucky if linked to an eight or a four.

Life is full of dangers.

Success, luck, happiness

Waiting, difficulty in getting the world

Honor, success and success

Late actions, danger

High success rate, luck

Long life, affection, support

Trials that end in success

Fear of those around you

Authority, power, intelligence

Danger of death, anguish

Unexpected danger, deception, trials

Neutral number that has the potential to be successful

General

Best if determined by instinct

Love, support, affection

Work hard and you will succeed

Fear

Power, authority as 27

Love, money, friendship

Mistrust, danger, uncertainties

The only way to get power is by working hard

General number

The key to success is to listen to your inner voice instead of relying on others

Love, affection and support Similar to 24 hours of love, affection and support.

Unfortunate events, failures, losses.

Risk of those close to you

Power and authority are easily accessible

Love, friendship and material success

Deception, grief - are like 44

Neutral number, success proportional to the amount of work done

Loneliness, isolation

The key to success is to use your instinct and not the advice of the majority

The luck of being a leader

Financial loss, failure unlucky life outcomes

It is not realistic to learn the Chaldean Numerology process overnight, however, if you choose to study this form further, you will reap many benefits.

Chinese Numerology

This is the first version of Numerology that we will see that has a history as the story of its birth. Legend has it that the Emperor of China Emperor Yu was able to see an animal shell with a grid of 9 squares that was perfectly uniform, and considered it to be a magic square. Because the turtle was found in the Lo River and the grid was named Lo Shu Square/ Grid. Lo Shu Square/ Grid. The ancient Chinese believed, some 4000 years ago, that number was at the base of all things.

The purpose of this grid is to multiply numbers vertically, horizontally or diagonally to create 15. This number was chosen because it is the exact number of days between the new moon day and the full moon day. The grid can be used to assess a person's strengths and traits in relation to their future development.

To use the grid, the month of birth is needed along with the year of birth and date of birth to determine that person's traits. It is essential to eliminate the zeros and only the numbers 1 through 9 are used. For example, if your birthday fell on July 5, 1983, you would write it as 7/5/1983, instead of 07/05/1983.

The frequency with which the same number appears in the year of birth also determines the character traits of a particular person. The list may be as follows.

1.

Occurs once: introvert

2. Occurs twice: communicative

Occurs three times: talkative

3. Occurs four times: four times Affectionate

Number 2

Occurs once: sensitive

Occurs twice: bright

Occurs three times: extremely sensitive

Occurs four times: lonely

3.

Occurs once: excellent

Occurs twice: creative

Occurs three times: imaginative

Occurs four times: overly imaginative

4.

Occurs once: stable and orderly

Occurs twice: pragmatic

Occurs three times: hard-working

Occurs four times: physical exercise

5

Occurs once: affectionate

Occurs twice: persistent

Occurs three times Determined

Four times: immediate actions

6.

Once is a good time to consult

Occurs twice: originating

Occurs three times: hot Temperate

Occurs four times: emotional

Number 7

Occurs once: learning experiences

Occurs twice: spiritual

Occurs three times: inclination to loss

Occurs four times: life difficulties

Number 8

Occurs once: meticulous

Occurs twice: inflexible

Occurs three times: materialistic Materialistic

Occurs four times: always on the move

Number 9

Occurs once: intelligent

Occurs twice: critical

Occurs three times: Givers

Occurs four times: bright, but lonely

The way to interpret the rows is as follows:

The top row of horizontals revolves around cerebral thinking, logic and reasoning, and imagination.

The middle row focuses on emotions and feelings, which include intuition and spirituality.

The bottom horizontal row focuses on athletic ability, practicality and common sense, as well as other physical elements.

The vertical row A focuses on action and sets things in motion.

The middle vertical row revolves around achievement, determination and perseverance.

The left vertical row focuses on the ability to think creatively, as well as intellectual capacity and the ability to perceive ideas.

Since both Astrology and Numerology are so closely interconnected, it is not surprising that Chinese Numerology uses Astrology's explanation of the five elements, Earth, Water, Fire, Metal and Wood. Each of the elements has its own set of associations that are helpful in keeping the zodiac symbol in mind when performing this type of numerology.

Earth: 8, 5, 2

Fire: 9

Water: 1

Metal: 7, 6

Wood: 4, 3

To place your numbers on the grid, follow these guidelines:

The number 9 is always placed in the upper right corner.

The number 8 appears in the middle of the right side.

The number 7 always appears at the bottom of the right side.

The number 6 always appears at the top of the center box.

5. The number 5 appears in the center.

The number 4 always appears located in the center of the lower square.

The number 3 always appears in the upper part of the left side.

The number 2 always appears in the middle of the left side.

The number 1 always appears at the bottom of the left side.

If you have more than two of the same number, then you will place them all inside the exact square. For example, if you were born on June 6, you would put the two 6's in the top center square. By interpreting the above numbers and rows, you may be able to determine your traits (or those of whomever the grid is for).

One thing to keep in mind is that there is a difference between the Western and Eastern interpretation of the numbers. You can choose either one to set your grid based on which one you feel more connected to. Because the Lo Shu grid is the Lo Shu grid can be described as heavily influenced by Eastern culture you may prefer to stick with the Eastern interpretations, however it is not necessary.

Below is an analysis of the Eastern and Western interpretations of each number, and their negative characteristics.

Number One

Eastern: moral, independent in their approach, and able to overcome obstacles.

Western: powerful, leaders, bosses, achievers, achievers.

Negatives: easy to become aggressive or angry

Number Two

Eastern: determination, luck

Western: unstoppable, powerful, calm, diplomatic, gentle persuasion

Positives: low self-esteem, extreme jealousy

Three

Eastern: abundance, growth

Western: bright, cheerful, social, friendly, optimistic

Negative aspects: scatterbrained, selfish

Fourth number

Eastern: struggles, difficulties

Western: reliable and hard-working, happy with the life of a simple man

Negative aspects: closed-minded, easily upset and determined to go their own way.

Five

Easterners The term "Eastern" can mean positive or negative, or balance.

Westerners are socially extroverted, energetic, active.

Negative aspects: inconsistent, unstable and addictive.

Sixth Number

Eastern: abundance, money

Westerners are compassionate, loving and kind. Peaceful, nurturing

Negative aspects include emotional guilt

Number Seven

Oriental: social, people skills, relational skills

Western Spiritual, charming, charming Deep thinker, fascinating

Negative aspects: withdrawn in their thoughts

Number Eight

Oriental Wealth, abundance True lucky number

Western: abundance, joy, strength, intelligence

Negative aspects: unwillingness to give, greed for money

Number Nine

Eastern Luck, happiness and long life

Western A mixture of positive traits, charming, imaginative and patient.

Negative aspects: know-it-all and insecure.

Abracadabra Numerology

This is the less popular type of Numerology that employs triangles to calculate numbers describing characters and events using the person's initial word. The values of the number given to the word Abracadabra

79

correspond to 365, which implies that it covers the whole year.

The triangles used in this form of numerology have their origin in Giza, Egypt, in the great pyramids that were built at Cheops. There is a belief that these ancient pyramids held ancient secrets, and this Inverted Triangle (or pyramid) is the basis of this method. The base of the triangle is the nine letters of the name, and or their numerical equivalents.

Abracadabra Numerology is a mysterious and mystical system that reveals the root number of a person's birth name and allows you to identify the traits that characterize him or her. The alphabetical translation of all Abracadabra Numerology numbers is available below.

A, J, S

B, K, T

C, L, U

D M V

E, N, W

F O, F, O

G P, Y

H, Q Z

I R

They should be similar to various types of Numerology that we have discussed in the previous sections. The most effective way to proceed from this point is to create tables showing the values of each letter. This allows you to look it up easily.

To begin, type in your initial name. Then, below each word, you should write the numbers from the tables or from the list above. Start adding the numbers on each line by putting them 2 by 2 so that each descending line has one less number than the line before it. All compound numbers should be reduced to single digits in the same way as we have been doing for most other types of Numerology. The only thing to do is to combine the two numbers. From this point on, you have to join all the single digit composite digits into lines, similar to how you did at the beginning. Each descending line has one less number than the previous one. Keep adding until there are single-digit numbers at the end in the triangle (the "dot"). The final number is your Abracadabra number.

Let's do an example together. Let's say the subject's name would be Ana. Here are the steps necessary to locate Anna's Abracadabra number.

A n n

1 5 5 1

6 6

12

3

The first thing we do is print Ana's name.

Next, we write the numbers corresponding to each letter.

Then we add them in two groups.

1 + 5, 5 + 1.

We have 6 and 6 in the next row.

On the other side, we add six and 6 which gives us 12 for the next row.

There is no way to get a two-digit number, so we have to add 1 + 2.

We are left with the Abracadabra number of three.

You may be thinking about what to do when you have names that don't contain an even number of letters, so let's set up an example for this scenario as well. Let's imagine that our subject name was Tiffany.

T i f f a n y

2 9 6 6 1 5 7

11 12 6 7

2 3 13

5 4

9

First, we print Tiffany's name.

Then, we write the numbers corresponding to each letter.

Next, we add the numbers in two groups. Then, we move the remaining seven to the bottom row, without altering the pattern.

The remaining numbers are 11 12, 6 and 7. To reduce the number of composite numbers, we multiply 1 + 1 1, 1 + 2 and 6 + 7.

This gives us 2, 3 and 13. To reduce the number of composite numbers, we multiply the sum of 2 and 3, as well as 1 plus 3. This leaves us with 5 and 4.

Next, we add these two numbers together, and we are left with the abracadabrante number 9.

There are many things that are not known about Abracadabra Numerology that may help explain why it is not the most commonly used type of Numerology.

Chapter 3: Discover Who You Are Supposed To Be A Step-By-Step Guide.

The natal chart, sometimes known as the birth chart is just a sketch of the sky, imagine yourself as the Moon, Sun, asteroids and planets at the exact moment you were born. According to astrologers and numerologists, the birth chart is the underlying outline of the life you have lived. It provides detailed insight into your personality weaknesses, as well as your strengths, habits, dislikes, desires and much more.

Your birth chart reveals your moon sign, sun signs, rising and falling sign, your homes, as well as the location of the planets during your birth, as well as the house in which you resided. It may offer a great deal of information as to why you act the way you do, or think about things the way you do or think the way you do, etc. The thing to keep in mind is that not all ideas are going to resonate with you, which is perfectly normal! Consider what you like and ignore the rest.

Using an astrological tracker, or a calculator available on websites, is the most convenient method of obtaining your birth chart. And it's usually free! There are many types of charts that serve different purposes. In this guide, we will focus on circle charts. The main advantage is that these sites provide a comprehensive description and breakdown of the entire chart, so you don't have to do any guesswork. Of course, it's advisable to drill down into areas you're unsure or uncertain about, but for the most part online calculators excel at explaining the entire chart in one place.

All you need to know to access your birth chart on your smartphone or computer are the following details about your personal information:

Date of birth

Month of birth

Year of birth

State of birth

Place of birth city

Hour of birth

Minute of birth

The reason it must be accurate is the fact that everything is in motion, which means that stars, planets and all things can change in the span of an hour. This could drastically alter your child's birth chart.

It is important not to be confused with the natal chart by the Life Path Numbers, Soul Impulse numbers or any other information. This information will be revealed later and will play into the birth chart, but they are not the main details of the birth chart. We will be able to find all of our primary numbers in later chapters.

It is also necessary to choose which house system you prefer to employ Although there are many options available, these are the most popular: Koch, Placidus and complete signs. In this guide, we will concentrate on Placidus because they produce an easy-to-follow, beginner-friendly chart.

After charting online (remember to select the circular chart as it is the easiest to understand) you will get a picture of your natal chart. Below that pictograph, you will get in-depth explanations for each section of your chart, usually starting with the sun sign.

This is a common way to read your birth chart:

Check your sun sign

Check your rising sign

Make sure you know your Moon sign

Check the houses in your birth chart

Check the planets in your chart and determine where they are.

Keep the entire chart in the back of your mind.

Certain aspects and meanings of your chart may seem strange when you look at it as an isolated piece of information. However, looking at the whole picture can make it easier to understand the situation and give you an accurate picture of your natal chart.

Sun sign

A person's Sun sign is their primary Zodiac. For those born on July 5, their sun sign is Cancer. The sun sign determines your personality as well as your primary characteristics as a person. It is the personality, their vital power and their imaginative capacity.

Moon Sign

Moon signs are the second most important element within our chart. The moon shows how we respond to situations, our patterns and how we feel when dealing with and expressing emotions. The moon shows us our inner desires to be at ease and shows us how to care for and nurture our body.

The Ascendant

The chart below will help you determine the first impression people are likely to have of your character, based on the energy you radiate. The Ascendant is a description of your physical health, your appearance and the type of 'social mask' we wear on the street. It also explains the defense mechanisms people use to adapt and cope with the world around them, as well as creating our initial impressions and expectations about the world.

The Descendant

It is completely opposite the Ascendant, and is also controlled by the opposite Zodiac that ruled the Ascendant. If, for example, your rising sign is Libra and your descending sign will be in Aries. This sign explains relationships as well as aspects of professional life.

Mercury

The planet you live on determines the way you make your decisions to communicate, share and exchange information. It helps you understand your reasoning and thinking, how you adapt to change and how you approach challenges.

Venus

This planet rules our values, our emotions and the things we like in our lives. Things like grace, charm and preferences for artistic trends, tastes and even beauty are controlled by Venus. If you are familiar with mythology, these concepts will be logical since Venus is known as the Roman goddess of love. Venus describes how we view relationships, and how we are attracted and drawn to things and people, as well as what we should invest our money in.

Mars

This planet is the one that regulates the need for violence, savagery and adventure and is the one that rules willpower. It is the exact opposite of Venus, peace, war, love, hate, feminine and masculine. Mars influences our emotions as well as our passions, our anger as well as our ability to defend ourselves and our confidence and how we deal with competition.

Jupiter

The planet we live on determines our beliefs. It helps us understand our goals and how we can achieve enlightenment and helps us explore our spiritual and intellectual realms. Jupiter also rules ethics and morals. This planet also affects our luck and good fortune and helps us achieve it depending on your particular Zodiac.

Saturn

This planet is responsible for order, responsibility and the need for conformity. Saturn is the one who determines what will be challenging in your life. It also reveals the things you must learn. You could think of Saturn as a taskmaster. His position indicates what areas of your life you should focus on to develop and improve. Saturn is known to have an unpopular reputation due to revealing your weaknesses more than your strengths, however, any growth, there is no way to grow without addressing your weaknesses. Therefore, Saturn could be considered one of the most important planets you have in your natal chart.

Uranus

This planet describes creativity, intelligence, originality and individuality. It helps you understand the extent to which you want to be able to make changes and also where you are most likely to break from the norm. Uranus determines the possibility that you prefer to be unattached for the rest of your life and somewhat forever young.

Neptune

This planet is strongly influenced by the impulse of emotions. It governs the perception of the ideal world and what it would be like. Neptune affects the senses and the imagination. Neptune is also the reason we feel and think about religions, and how we believe in the higher gods.

Pluto

This planet is ruled by change, purging and destruction, and creation. It is death, rebirth and transformation all at once. Pluto helps you discover the source of your energy and whether you are willing to let it go. Pluto determines the difficult choices between your worries and your ultimate joy. Pluto also has a say over money and sexuality.

Zodiac signs, meanings and signs in your natal chart.

As mentioned above, we all have different zodiac signs that add up to our primary sign (sun). This is due to the fact that astrologers of earlier times divided the sky into twelve parts which are The 12 zodiac signs form the Zodiac. The purpose of the Zodiacs in your birth chart The Zodiacs within your birth charts is to incorporate the characteristics of the sign into the houses, planets and other places where the signs reside.

Aquarius: January 20 to February 18

Eccentric, rebellious, emotional detachment, progressive, collaborative.

Pisces: February 19 to March 20

Intuitive healing, unconscious dreaming, sensitive spiritual.

Aries: March 21 to April 19

New beginnings are always instigating, courageous, strong and passionate. It is a spontaneous and unplanned process.

Taurus: April 20 to May 20

Practical, sensual, persistent, practical, reliable, physical, finances, abundance.

Gemini: May 21 to June 20

Connective, ideas, communicative, sociable, restless, changeable, fast-moving

Cancer: May 22-June 22

Sensitive, nurturing, emotional, maternal, home, nurturing, intuitive feminine

Leo July 23 - August 22

Love, courage, self-expression and generosity, loyalty, imagination and empowerment.

Virgo August 23 to September 22

Practical, well organized and efficient, service and health oriented. Analytical, analytical,

Libra September 23 to October 22

Beauty, fairness, diplomacy Balance, equality, love and focus on aesthetics.

Scorpio November 22 to 21

Intimacy, depth mystery, power sex, possession, money transformation

Sagittarius November 22 to December 21

Expansive knowledge, adventure, learning and philosophical teaching

Capricorn: December 22 to January 19

Commitment to investing, maturity, goals for financial future, rewards.

The twelve houses of the zodiac

There are 12 houses within Astrology, from the First House to the Twelfth House. Each has its own importance and is controlled by a particular Zodiac.

First House

This house is the beginning of the Zodiac and is the home of all the "first times". That is, appearance, self-image, first impressions, new beginnings, new ideas, etc. The house is of the cusp signs, which represents the ascendant.

The ruler of: Aries

Second House

This house includes things related to your physical and environmental surroundings: think of the five senses, hearing, touch and smell. This house rules income, money and self-esteem.

The ruler is Taurus.

Third House

The house of communication encompasses all forms, including conversations, thinking devices, gadgets and other devices, as well as neighbors, siblings, libraries and travel schools, community events and teachers.

Gemini is the ruler of Gemini.

Fourth House

The house is the foundation of everything. It is the place of intimacy, family, home, parental security, parenting and children.

It is the main cause of cancer.

Fifth House

The house is filled with the power of color, drama self-expression, attention love, imagination, romance and fun.

The ruler of: Leo

Sixth House

This house is an overview of everything related to health and service. It includes routines, schedules, food organization and exercise, healthy living and natural living. It also encompasses services to others.

Ruled by Virgo

Seventh House

This house encompasses others and relationships. It encompasses personal relationships, as well as business partnerships, marriage contracts, business agreements and other relationship matters.

Ruled by: Libra

Eighth House

The house of the dead is a symbol of the mystery of life: death and birth, transformation merging energies, mystery, bonds and sex. It also rules money and the property of others, including inheritances, investments and real estate.

Scorpio is the ruler. Scorpio

Ninth House

This house includes expansion, long distance travel as well as inspiration, foreign language the mind, publishing, higher education optimism, motivation and risk, adventure, luck gambling, religion, ethics morality, philosophy and ethics.

Ruled by Sagittarius

Tenth House

This house is the reflection of the public aspects of our life. It governs structures, corporations as well as honors, traditions as well as awards, achievements and discipline as well as rules and boundaries, authority as well as parenthood, and also fame. The house also houses a cusp sign and a midheaven sign, which provides clues to your profession.

Capricorn is the ruler of Capricorn.

Eleventh House

This house encompasses friendships, society, technological equipment, friendships, electronic media, as well as human rights, social justice networks and the idea of rebellion. It also includes surprise, wonder, ingenuity, innovation, science fiction, sudden events and the science of astronomy.

Ruled by: Aquarius

Twelfth House

This house closes the Zodiac, making it the symbol par excellence of endings. It is the house of finality, of old age, of tying up loose ends, of the end of a task and of surrender. It also encompasses matters that require isolation from society, such as hospitals and institutions, enemies and prisons. The final elements of which this house is a part are cinema, creative imagination, art journals and magazines, dance, the unconscious and poetry.

The ruler of Pisces is: Pisces.

House systems

In this chapter we have discussed the three main house systems which are Koch, Placidus and the whole house. However, there are more than fifteen house systems that can be used. To simplify things, this chapter will focus on Koch, Placidus, the whole house and Equal.

Koch

The house system is based on the horizon lines at different times of day on your birthday. It calculates how long the MC degree of the zodiac has been above the horizon since it rose. Simply put, this system is a way of separating the motions of the planets so that it is a time-oriented system.

Placidus

The house system also separates the movement of the stellar and planetary phases, both above and below the horizon. It is a time-oriented system, much like the Koch system.

Full house

The system gives each Zodiac its own house. This means that each house is an independent house. The first house is that of the Zodiac with the ascendant we discussed in the previous section. Each Zodiac follows its own path and fills an entire house, rather than being shared in other systems. This system is part of the group of equal houses.

Equality

Like the whole house system, in the sense that the group that is this group takes the ascendant as the cusp of that of the First House. All houses are equal by precisely 30 degrees to each other. That means that the Tenth House point does not correspond to the MC, but is identical to the ascendant, making it the apical point of the Zodiac above the horizon.

Using a professional astrologer

There are definitely benefits to using an online calculator particularly if you are interested about their design and the information they provide however, can seem confusing. This is especially true if you are first time trying to read the chart. The information you get from your letter will not do you much good, especially in case you have any doubts. This is the time to consult an astrologer.

Not only can they design your chart, but they can guide you through every aspect of your chart and answer any questions you may have. They can focus on specific areas or even the whole thing: you decide. Professional astrologers can be expensive, but they usually cost half an hour and, if you are interested in your birth chart, can be a valuable experience.

Chapter 4: Analyzing Famous People's Birth Charts

Once you know the basics of reading a birth chart, it's time to apply it in the real world. We will look at some of the most famous birth charts and review the different sections.

Diana of Wales Princess Diana of Wales

Princess Diana was born on July 1, 1961 at 19:45 in Sandringham, United Kingdom.

Diana's Sun is in Cancer. People with the sun sign Cancer generally tend to remain intimate and tend to avoid sharing their personal lives with others, and are more likely to reminisce about their past. They tend to have an unpopular reputation as moody people, who hold back change and seek security and comfort in everything they do. They are often classified as old souls and have an aversion to historical objects, such as old photographs and antiques.

Diana's Ascendant is in Sagittarius. People with their Ascendant in Sagittarius tend to look for an exciting world ahead, are open to something new and believe in the power of faith and hope. They are always looking for something. This can be a problem, as it can lead them to become dissatisfied. They will always make their own opinions known and can be extremely outspoken.

Diana's Moon is in Aquarius. People who have their Moon within Aquarius are generally extremely aware of their surroundings. They are dedicated to studying human nature and are usually able to analyze why and the reasons why people do what they do. They are generally considered to be very independent, and are likely to be extremely strong-willed and rebellious with more conservative beliefs.

Diana is a victim of Mercury in Cancer. People with Mercury in Cancer tend to speak with a sensitive, reflective and withdrawn personality. They are not as outgoing, regardless of their natal chart, but tend to be very personal. They are recognized as very deep thinkers who are of introspection and meditation.

Diana is Venus placed in Taurus. People with Venus in Taurus are generally secure and comfortable. They tend to require an element of reliability and predictability in their relationships and may feel threatened by intense situations concerning the love of their lives and their relationships. One of their shortcomings could be that they can be too settled and resist the need for change in their relationships. They are not usually as easily influenced by the words they say as they are by their actions.

Diana is Mars in Virgo. People born with Mars in Virgo tend to be very busy and practical, as well as goal-oriented and efficient. However, they can end up feeling scattered, although they tend to be able to multitask and also accomplish many tasks at the same time and with ease. They can be a bit negative at times, but they don't usually make others feel uncomfortable. They are known as a big nag when they are upset However, these cases do not last long.

Diana is Jupiter in Aquarius. People with Jupiter in Aquarius generally have the most favorable outcomes when they are creative, compassionate and cooperative. They are also fair, even-handed and equitable. They are able to decide when to think outside the norm and break the rules. The freedom of the individual is highly valued.

Diana is Saturn placed in Capricorn. People with Saturn in Capricorn tend to appreciate being treated with respect and being appreciated by others. They tend to overcome obstacles more easily than others because of their patience. They tend to be highly motivated and have a passion for success.

Diana is born with Uranus in Leo. People with Uranus in Leo tend to drastically change their styles, art, theater, etc. and appreciate the ability to express themselves freely. They tend to seek progress, but may have a negative image for sticking to their lifestyle.

Diana is Neptune in Scorpio. People with Neptune in Scorpio tend to believe that when people can understand each other or try to understand each other, the ideal world will come true. They believe in accepting everyone equally, regardless of their background. They are also of the opinion that transition and transformation is the best method of bringing about change.

Diana is Pluto placed in Virgo. People with Pluto in Virgo often feel dissatisfied in self-care routines, at work, as well as in health, wellness or service. It is essential for them to keep in mind that power comes from loving these activities and not trying to get that level of love by doing these things. They are likely to have fantastic ideas for healing the body and mind.

Diana's Sun is in the seventh house. People in this house tend to create harmony and manage their relationships very well. They tend to want to be liked and do not handle rejection well. The downside of this can be that they feel unfinished without a partner, identify too much with other people, and are not sensitive enough to the opinions of those around them in their personal preferences. They tend to be very adept at bringing out the best in people, seeking balance and harmony, and being able to compromise often.

Diana's Moon is in House II. People in House II tend to go from saving funds one day to being reckless the next. However, they will make sure their bills are paid, as it gives them a sense of security. They tend to be reckless with their spending more often when they are anxious or emotionally angry.

Diana is a Mercury sign located in Mercury is in the seventh house. People in this sign tend to enjoy debates because they can help make the right decisions. They do so because the ability to make a decision can be challenging for them because they tend to consider both perspectives or possibilities and find the value in them. However, while they may require interactions with others, they rarely adhere to the advice of others, preferring to follow their own course.

Diana is Venus in House V. They are flirtatious, romantic, sensual and love all things. They love to be the center of attention and are constantly captivated by something or someone. They tend to be charming, trusting and warm. They are wonderful company.

Diana is born with Mars placed in the Eighth House. People of this sign tend to feel passion in a lively and magical way. They excel in research and study, psychology or any other project they are passionate about. The passion that drives them is what keeps them awake and out of bed.

Diana is a Jupiter sign located in the Second House of Jupiter. They tend to be extremely creative, which leads people to believe that they are lucky with possessions or gifts, as well as money. They are extremely comfortable and can be found to indulge themselves.

Diana is born with Saturn within the I House of Saturn. They are extremely responsible, but find it difficult to free themselves from this obligation. They are often unsure of their choices and often turn to family and friends for help.

Diana is Uranus in Uranus is in the Eighth House. People born in the Eighth House tend to go against the grain, embracing freedom of expression rather than the usual adherence to rules.

Diana is Neptune within the Tenth House. People with this personality type usually have an excellent sense of business trends, fashions, as well as public appeal. They typically have a vision, a sense of humor, and a love of artistic talent for their work.

Diana is ruled by Pluto within the Eighth House. They are attracted to the dark side and it often leads them to experiences that others may not experience. They also like control of their finances and may have financial problems with their spouses.

Winston Churchill

Winston Churchill was born on November 30, 1874 at around 13:30, in Woodstock, UK.

Winston Churchill's Sun is in Sagittarius. People with the Sun in Sagittarius are generally reliable, flexible and positive. They are also social, inclined to optimism and are honest.

Winston Churchill's Ascendant is Libra. People with the Ascendant in Libra tend to

Winston Churchill's Moon is in Leo. People with Moon in Leo tend to be generous tender, loving and affectionate. They don't do well being overlooked.

Winston Churchill has Mercury in Scorpio. People with Mercury in Scorpio tend to be extremely focused and love to decipher issues, as well as focus on physical pursuits and sexual desires.

Winston Churchill has Venus in Sagittarius. People with Venus in Sagittarius tend to like new experiences, travel, and experiences in the arts and culture.

Winston Churchill has Mars in Libra. People with Mars in Libra tend to be at a crossroads between being assertive and assertive to get their own way or keeping the peace by changing their personal beliefs, morals or convictions.

Winston Churchill has Jupiter in Libra. People with Jupiter in Libra are typically social, philosophically inspired, compassionate and inspirational. They tend to like visually appealing things and are interested in art and art-related activities.

Winston Churchill has Saturn in Aquarius. People with Saturn in Aquarius tend to have strong resilience and an awareness of humanity in general, but less so on an individual scale. They are prone to think outside the box and generally have a new vision.

Winston Churchill has Uranus in Leo. People with Uranus in Leo tend to be unaffected by traditions. They are bold, imaginative and are able to come up with new concepts.

Winston Churchill has Neptune in Aries. People with Neptune in Aries tend to be inquisitive, courageous, spontaneous creative and skilled in organization.

Winston Churchill has Pluto in Taurus. People with Pluto in Taurus tend to have a regular process of completing projects. They require time to think about their choices that are practical and rational and are able to accomplish a task over long periods of time.

Winston Churchill has the Sun in House III. People in the Third House tend to enjoy assimilating new knowledge, compiling it and sharing the new information with others.

Winston Churchill has the Moon in the Eleventh House. People with this sign tend to have a desire to be part of the group more than others. They are enthusiastic about helping other people, social networking and charity work.

Winston Churchill has Mercury in the Second House. People in the Second House tend to think about the financial situation and can be very expressive, both in the written and spoken word.

Winston Churchill has Venus in the Third House. They are skilled in writing and creative communication They also dislike conflict.

Winston Churchill has Mars in the First House. They tend to have a lot of physical energy which can lead to recklessness. They are confident and self-assured, as well as excellent organizers.

120

Winston Churchill has Jupiter in the First House. These individuals tend to be exceptional leaders and are able to bring faith to people with a positive outlook. They tend to be enthusiastic about sports, the outdoors, and indulgence.

Winston Churchill has Saturn in the Fifth House. People with Saturn in the Fifth House are often inadequate in relationships and receive an unpopular reputation for being aloof, indifferent and distant in their speech. They usually only engage in activities that are beneficial to the person in one way or another.

Winston Churchill has Uranus in the Eleventh House. People with Uranus tend to be friends with people who are innovative, original creative, artistic or ingenious in some way.

Winston Churchill has Neptune in the Eighth House. People with this personality type tend to have an intuitive sense and are more attuned to the spiritual realm: dreams that show the future or have premonitions.

Winston Churchill has Pluto in the Eighth House. They are skilled in intelligent analysis, courageous and astute. They have a clear sense that can be used in business, although they could have certain financial difficulties.

Adolf Hitler

Adolf Hitler was born on April 20, 1889, at the age of 1830. He lived in Braunau am Inn, Austria.

Adolf Hitler's Sun is in Taurus. People with the Sun in Taurus tend to be determined, hard-working and realistic. They are also sensitive, compassionate, trustworthy and reliable. They are comfortable with routines as long as they are beneficial.

Adolf Hitler's Ascendant lives in Libra. People with their Ascendant in Libra tend to be charming and polite. They are sophisticated, elegant charming, graceful diplomats, charming and creative. They are also friendly and sociable. They are prone to avoid conflict and quite impulsive, as well as being more susceptible to selfishness and giving a lot of weight to appearances.

Adolf Hitler's Moon is in Capricorn. People with their Moon in Capricorn tend to be more quiet and reserved. They may not be comfortable with emotional expressions of love, making it difficult to ask for and/or accept help.

Adolf Hitler has Mercury in Aries. People with Mercury in Aries tend to speak their mind and can be competitive and argumentative. They may also have an active mind.

Adolf Hitler has Venus in Taurus. People who have Venus placed in Taurus tend to be emotionally reliable, warm and loyal in their love relationships. They are prone to the top and to give too much importance to the aesthetic and material aspects of things.

Adolf Hitler has Mars in Taurus. People with Mars in Taurus are usually very determined. If they set their mind to something, they will do anything to get it.

Adolf Hitler has Jupiter in Capricorn. People with Jupiter in Capricorn tend to be confident in their abilities, resourceful and authentic. They may experience restrictions, or reservations, and the need to purchase tangible items.

Adolf Hitler has Saturn in Leo. People with Saturn in Leo tend to be powerful leaders with the ability to be diplomatic. They are traditional, competent and independent. They are also organized. Some may think they are indifferent or a mystery.

Adolf Hitler's Sun is in House VII. They tend to choose people of the highest social scale, who are respected and able to boost their social standing. A congenial and trustworthy partner is essential, as well as having someone who can help the person with their own strength and abilities.

Adolf Hitler's Moon is in House III. They tend to be flexible, curious and seek the thrill of the unexpected. They are always looking for ways to entertain themselves.

Adolf Hitler has Mercury in the Seventh House. They are known to seek partners with a good education and outstanding intelligence. Being able to engage in intelligent conversations is a great attraction.

Adolf Hitler has Venus in the Seventh House. They are generally charming, enjoy social interaction and have the ability to connect with others.

Adolf Hitler has Mars in House VII. They are stubborn and independent, and often demand that things work their way. They can make people feel that they are rude and unkind.

Adolf Hitler has Jupiter in the Third House. They don't usually have trouble seeing the big picture, but tend to be unaware of particular aspects. They tend to be somewhat more conservative, however, they are also cautious.

Adolf Hitler has Saturn in the Tenth House. They tend to be independent, disciplined with structure and have a strong business mentality. They are capable of a slow climb to success, not an explosive leap.

Adolf Hitler has Uranus in the Twelfth House. They tend to be optimists who prefer to be in the shadows and possess an innate sense of.

Adolf Hitler has Neptune in the Eighth House. People with Neptune in the Eighth House are prone to dreamlike visions and premonitions, and may have dreams that reveal their future.

Adolf Hitler has Pluto in the Eighth House. People of this sign tend to excel in analysis, are courageous and shrewd. Their insight can be beneficial in their business dealings, but they may have financial problems in their personal or business relationships.

Bruce Lee

Bruce Lee was born on November 27, 1940 at around 7:12 am located in San Francisco, California.

Bruce Lee's Sun is in Sagittarius. People with the Sun in Sagittarius tend to be optimistic, open, honest, flexible, trustworthy and idealistic. However, they can also be aggressive, selfish or obsessive. They are also unyielding, arrogant and narrow-minded.

Bruce Lee's Ascendant is in Sagittarius. People with their Ascendant in Sagittarius tend to be religious, socially active, easy-going, adventurous and optimistic. They can also be narrow-minded and rigid, as well as risk-averse and even phony.

Bruce Lee's Moon is in Scorpio. People with Moon in Scorpio tend to be more reserved in their thoughts, distrustful of other people, and have difficulty with emotional intimacy.

Bruce Lee has Mercury in Scorpio. People with Mercury in Scorpio tend to have great concentration, decoding and analytical abilities, and are extremely perceptive and attentive.

Bruce Lee has Venus in Scorpio. People who have Venus in Scorpio tend to form attachments that are intense and emotional, yet they may feel a desire to be in control and jealous of their loved ones.

Bruce Lee has Mars in Scorpio. People with Mars in Scorpio tend to have strong determination, are goal-focused and have strong control and determination. They tend to be inflexible when they have opinions and are difficult to change.

Bruce Lee has Jupiter in Taurus. People with Jupiter in Taurus tend to favor material trade-offs for the benefit of humanity using specific strategies. Their values are not easily changed.

Bruce Lee has Saturn in Taurus. People born with Saturn placed in Taurus are reliable and hardworking, as well as cautious and self-controlled. They are also well-prepared, organized and persistent.

Bruce Lee's Sun is in the Twelfth House. People in this house tend to work for humanity, with an innate sense of purpose.

Bruce Lee's Moon is in the Eleventh House. People with this sign tend to have strong relationships with women and place great importance on how they are perceived by social settings.

Bruce Lee has Mercury in the Eleventh House. People with Mercury in this house tend to be flexible, easy-going, naive and able to handle unpredictable situations. They tend to have great determination to pursue goals that require intellect.

Bruce Lee has Venus in the 11th House. They are friendly, open, welcoming and social.

Bruce Lee has Mars in the Eleventh House. They are the ones who direct events and invest a lot of energy in relationships and friendships, but they also have the potential to take advantage of others or be victims of.

Bruce Lee has Jupiter in the Fifth House. They tend to be fortunate when it comes to romantic relationships and with their children. They tend to be optimistic, cheerful and are in awe of the opportunity to educate others.

Bruce Lee has Saturn in the Fifth House. They tend to be emotionally distant and may wish to be viewed with more respect by others than they really are.

Bruce Lee has Uranus in the Sixth House. People with Uranus tend to be self-sufficient, intelligent and able to work independently. Most jobs are boring, as interacting with colleagues and being patient with them is not an area of strength for them.

Bruce Lee has Neptune in the Tenth House. People with Neptune often have a different career path, which could result in unrealistic goals or beliefs related to their accomplishments.

Bruce Lee has Pluto in the Eighth House. They tend to be intelligent, self-confident, and adept at analysis. They may have a sixth sense that helps them excel in business.

Steve Jobs

Steve Jobs was born on February 24, 1955, when he was 19 years old, and on February 24 in San Francisco, California.

Steve Jobs' Sun is in Pisces. People with the Sun in Pisces tend to relate to other people, are adaptable and have extremely open minds. They can be seen as apathetic, however it is usually just their desire for a greater goal and a higher level of transcendence.

Steve Jobs' Ascendant is in Virgo. People with their Ascendant in Virgo are usually quiet, intelligent and shy, and tend to overthink things. People may consider them aloof or cold.

Steve Jobs' Moon is in Aries. People who have their Moon in Aries usually have intense passion or fire within them and have no difficulty managing their emotions. They have what they want and will not be patient.

Steve Jobs has Mercury in Aquarius. People who have Mercury in Aquarius generally exhibit a unique style, unafraid to break the rules and providing an alternative perspective compared to the standard.

Steve Jobs has Venus in Capricorn. People with Venus in Capricorn are usually able to demonstrate excellent self-control, responsible behavior, and a clear and calm mind. They may not express feelings of love often, and tend to give the impression of being unloving. However, they can be romantic with the right person.

Steve Jobs has Mars in Aries. People with Mars in Aries tend to be quick, impulsive, forward-looking and active. They are able to trust their intuitions and tend to accomplish a lot this way.

Steve Jobs has Jupiter in Cancer. People with Jupiter in Cancer are usually lucky and are generous, compassionate and comforting to those around them. They are inclined to appreciate traditions and seek the security of their homes.

Steve Jobs has Saturn in Scorpio. People with Saturn in Scorpio generally have a focused and strong will. They are stubborn, brutal and will endure anything to achieve their goals.

Steve Jobs has Uranus in Cancer. People with Uranus in Cancer are usually looking for new ideas, updating old ways of life, making adjustments, as well as having routines at home.

Steve Jobs has Neptune in Libra. People who have Neptune placed in Libra have their ideal vision about the world, which is fairness among people. They might idealize peace, harmony, cooperation and relationships and are prone to not judge other people.

Steve Jobs has Pluto in Leo. People with Pluto in Leo are often prone to intense emotions about self-expression, romance and love, as well as children, plus creativity and destiny.

Steve Jobs has the Sun in the Sixth House. They tend to need positive criticism for what they have accomplished and find it difficult not to over-identify with the opinions of others.

Steve Jobs has the Moon in the Seventh House. People of this sign tend to need emotional connections in their relationships. They tend not to accomplish things on their own and find satisfaction in their relationships.

Steve Jobs has Mercury in the Fifth House. People with Mercury tend to be creative and make use of their voice, whether written or spoken, to convey their ideas. They tend to be entertaining, engaging, funny and humorous.

Steve Jobs has Venus in the Fourth House. They tend to seek harmony, peace, beauty and harmony in their personal and domestic life. They tend to enjoy home activities and are affectionate, compassionate and loving.

Steve Jobs has Mars in the Eighth House. People of this sign tend to be captivated by passion and magically avoid betrayal, as well as go to great lengths to carry out the projects they love.

Steve Jobs has Jupiter in the Tenth House. These individuals tend to approach situations with a kind and assertive personality. They are naturally talented, intelligent, ethical and mature.

Steve Jobs has Saturn in the Third House. People with Saturn in the Third House tend to have an extremely high degree of endurance and perseverance, which is advantageous as they may experience a break in their education.

Steve Jobs has Uranus in the Tenth House. These are people who value their life as meaningful and continually strive to improve their quality of life.

Steve Jobs has Neptune in the Second House. They do not place value on the money they earn, and are likely to succeed through the pursuit of art.

Steve Jobs has Pluto in the Twelfth House. They tend to probe into the deeper meaning of things by analyzing their psychological makeup and even their dreams. They show a lot of empathy and are often able to help others.

Chapter 5: Understanding Your True Self Using Pythagorean Arrows

Pythagorean Arrows are a type of arithmetic using grids. They are also known as Complete Number Planes. Pythagorean Arrows are also known in the field of Complete Number Lines or Complete Number Planes and are like the Lo Shu square that we have discussed with Chinese Numerology. The arrows provide insight into certain characteristics and personality traits. If combined with other calculations, strong positive and negative characteristics of a person can be identified.

The grid used in The Arrows and Arrows of Pythagoras has a 3x3 grid, which means it is composed of 9 squares. The layout is as follows:

The square on the right is 7.

The middle square is 8

The right square is 9

The bottom middle square is 4

In the middle is 5

The top middle square is 6

The left square is 1

The middle square on the left is 2

The left side of the top square is 3

The bottom row represents the physical plane, while the middle row is the emotional plane, while the top row shows the mental plane. There are eight different positive arrows, as well as 7 negative arrows.

Positive arrows

Planner Arrows Planner Arrows: 1, 2 and 3.

They are excellent at organizing, planning and understanding their goals. However, they often overthink things, which can lead to a lack of enjoyment.

Willpower Arrow: 4, 3, 5 and 6.

They are persistent and get carried away, which can lead to a stubborn cut-off that can be rude to other people. They are extremely determined and tend to achieve their goals and dreams.

Activity Arrow Activity Arrow: 7, 8 and 9

They are active, energetic and restless. They are driven to be constantly active.

Determination Arrow: 1, 5 and 9

These individuals are determined, ambitious and determined. They do not let difficulties stand in their way, effortlessly overcoming obstacles to achieve success.

Arrow of Practicality: 1 7, 4 and 1

They are down to earth, practical and persevering. They are driven by the physical things they have and work in a visual or practical way, especially using their hands.

Arrow of Emotions: 2, 5 and 8

They are committed and intense, and some of them lean toward the dramatic, which can make them excellent performers.

Intellect Arrow: 3, 6 and 9

These individuals are intelligent with an impressive memory. They can be lazy due to their lack of interest in not being able to use their full potential.

Arrow of Compassion: 3, 5 and 7

They are tolerant of both the highs and lows of their lives, while appearing to have peace within themselves. They are typically philosophers or musicians with a fascination for spirituality and mysticism, the occult as well as psychic art.

Negative Arrows

Frustration Arrow: 4 6, 5 and 4

People like this tend to expect the same from others, which can lead to disappointment because of their expectations.

Inactivity Arrow Inactivity Arrow: 9, 8 and 7.

They have little or no reason to live and often need motivation to achieve. They are slow to decide by analyzing their options before making a decision.

Impracticality Arrow: 1 3, 4 and 7

These individuals are unrealistic and tend to be idealistic, which causes them difficulties in daily life. They tend to be chaotic.

The Arrow of Sensitivity 2,5 and 8.

They are easily hurt and are incredibly sensitive to the opinions of others and are prone to withdraw from difficult situations.

Arrows of Bad Memory: 3, 6 and 9.

They are uninformed and forgetful, but intelligent.

Arrow of Resignation: 1, 5 and 9

These are people who cannot overcome their lack of determination or motivation. They lack perseverance, determination and motivation. Their dedication to work requires work and they need encouragement to complete their projects.

Skepticism Arrow 3, 5 and 7

These people have a hard time trusting people and seek to see proof in order to believe in them.

To fill in your grid, start with your name along with your date of birth, your name and address at the top. It is best to make use of your date of birth to determine the grid numbers and will not include zeros and 0s.

Chapter 6: How To Encrypt The Secret Vibrations Of Your Date Of Birth

We have discovered that each number that relates to us possesses a particular resonance and energy, as well as a meaning, so it is natural that the most significant of these is our children's date of birth. The date we were born on is certain dates in certain months in particular years for particular reasons - all of these aspects pertain to the force of nature that helps us to follow our own personal path.

There are many things we can identify using the date of birth of our children. If we take the whole set of numbers we get the Life Path Number (sometimes called the Fate Number). It is the one that carries the most weight over all the numbers associated with it, as it represents the direction of our life and what the universe has in store for us based on our interests and profession and the experiences we have and the people we know and the possibilities we possess. One fascinating thing to keep in mind is that the impact of this Life

Path Number leads is usually most significant when we reach the age of 35.

It is possible to have 11 Life Path Numbers that anyone can be blessed with, and you can read their descriptions below.

One: They tend to be self-confident and hold their beliefs in their individuality. They are leaders and pioneers who believe in their abilities and their ideas. They are different and are not afraid to follow their own path in life regardless of the rules that seem to be imposed on other people. However, this does not mean that it will not involve a battle, so it is essential for them to stick to their goals and not conform to the rules.

Two: they often find that their destiny is revealed in the relationships they have with others. That means they tend to be peacemakers and diplomats who are cautious, persistent and subtle in achieving their goals. They thrive when working with teams that have individuals with strong determination. They excel when they are patient and focused.

Three: These individuals are destined to succeed through the development of communication and interpersonal skills. They can easily inspire others and frequently impress others, which translates into happiness within their own lives. With their charm, charismatic creativity and artistic flair with their words, they can find success. They perform in a variety of ways and do not allow that flexibility to diminish or impede their enthusiasm.

Four: They achieve their goals through commitment to work, effort and self-control. They thrive in situations where they can find a logical approach to dealing with facts rather than opinions. They are often known for their ability to complete tasks effectively. Using the right combination of hard work, routine efficiency, reliability and service can lead to their achievement.

Five: The purpose of these individuals is to experience and gain from the changes and experiences taking place within their own lives. They are fluid and must learn to make the most of their freedom. They will succeed if they do not tie themselves down to too many obligations and run the risk of becoming bored or dissatisfied. They are successful when they take advantage of the opportunities presented to them.

Six: They find their purpose in service to others, and that includes responsibility and the well-being of other people. It can be in the workplace or at home and they have to manage a whole group, which makes them efficient and supportive. They excel at empowering the less capable, taking care of them, and putting the interests of others before their own. They achieve their goals through determination and support.

Seven: These individuals will discover their purpose in the search for the mental and spiritual aspects of the purpose of existence. Loneliness is a crucial factor for these individuals because it is essential for the growth of these regions. People who have superficial relationships are not compatible with them or with family relationships. Studying and working in the sciences or philosophy can bring the success they desire.

Eight: These individuals are likely to find their way in commerce, as long as they are profitable and committed. They are leaders by nature, with a sense of vision, power of attraction, and the ability to influence people and things to benefit themselves. They can achieve success if they understand how to take advantage of situations through gaining allies in places of high power.

Nine: These individuals will discover their purpose in expanding the scope of consciousness and understanding for humans. They will be successful performing artistic activities as it allows them to convey universal truths. They will enjoy emotional interactions with a wide variety of people. They will see the world from a broad and philosophical perspective without prejudice. They will be able to inspire others.

Master Number Eleven (2) These individuals are blessed with a unique destiny. They have a good chance of having a positive impact on many people, and possibly even gaining fame. They have an innate sense of intuition that, when developed, can inspire others. However, the downside is that they can be unbalanced. They can be successful in finding a balance between practicality and irrational thinking. It is easier to focus first on the frequency lower than 2 (diminished 11) to fully realize the potential of the master number.

Master Number Twenty-two (4) The persons indicated are destined to have a unique and special destiny. They are capable of immense influence and power which they will have to manage with care. They can be the cause of massive destruction or of much creativity. They have to learn to act in the interests of others, using their resources to benefit others rather than the bad guys. They will succeed in transforming the world if they focus on their goals and bring change.

How to find your life path number

To determine your life path number, you will need the date, month and year you were born. Then, you'll add them together and reduce those numbers to a single digit in case it's not one of the two master digits (11 or 22).

Examples

Let's say our subject's birthday falls on July 5, 1986.

07/05/1986

At first, we want to reduce the length of the year.

$1 + 9 + 8 + 6 = 24$

Next, we include the month and day.

24 + 7 + 5 = 36

3 + 6 = 9

For this person it is 9.

Let's say the next example we will talk about was born on the 29th of 1953.

12/29/1953

The first step is to reduce the length of the year.

1 + 9 + 5 + 3 = 18

Then, we include that in the month and day.

18 + 1 + 2 + 2 + 9 = 32

3 + 2 = 5

For this particular person it is 5.

Let's say our last example was born on November 5, 1986.

11/05/1986

At first, we want to reduce the length of the year.

1 + 9 + 8 + 6 = 24

Then, we include it in the month and day.

24 + 1 + 1 + 5 = 31

3 + 1 = 4

The life path number for this individual would be 4.

In our last example let's say the subject's birthday falls on August 4, 1961.

08/04/1961

The first step is to reduce the length of the year.

1 + 9 + 6 + 1 = 17

Next, we include the month and day.

17 + 8 + 4 = 29

2 + 9 = 11

Since 11 is a master number, we do not reduce it any further than that and this means that the individual's life path number is 11.

The Day of Birth Number

The day of our birth date can give us an overview of who we are and how we see ourselves. If you remember that time we reviewed the birth chart for Astrology The Sun was the primary factor in the chart, and the Moon was the second. The same goes for your life path number, as well as your birth day number. It can provide insight into our childhood life, as well as the skills, talents and abilities we received as children. It is also a good indicator of our age. The birth day number can also help us decide our future job. An interesting fact to keep in mind is the fact that this particular number has the greatest influence between the ages of 28 and 56.

Some numerologists value both the full number and the reduced version (15 can also be 6) However, the most accurate interpretation is always derived from the full day. Each of the 31 birth day numbers is explained below.

They are usually the center of attention due to an energetic personality. Choosing an artistic career could bring success to the one who chooses it, as they can explore their interests in a unique way. Another possibility is to work with children or pets to understand their sensitive and emotional side. They will succeed on their own or as leaders, because they like things the way they want them to be.

These people tend to communicate with others more on an emotional level than on an intellectual level, because they possess a great capacity for perception. They are usually the most successful in management, politics or other related fields, because they excel at controlling other people. They enjoy working closely.

These people are extremely patient and tolerant of people who are different from them. As a result, they can easily adapt to more complicated issues and often pass this ability on to their colleagues. They are successful in the field of theology, as well as in travel, educational publishing or finance.

They tend to be very energetic and are happy to harness and channel energy to achieve their goals. They have a lot of freedom in their professional lives and love to take credit for their own successes, as they like to be the boss, not participating in group activities unless they are the person in charge.

They are people who are interested in thinking of new ideas using an analytical approach because it interests them. They excel in positions where they are hands-on or quick to think, such as administration, computer therapy, accounting, or computer science.

They are effortlessly friendly, which allows them to be personable and make strong connections. They are able to find jobs that allow them to show their love of art or music, or that enable them to work closely with others, such as a lawyer, consultant or representative or advisor.

They have high standards and may be disappointed when others do not meet their expectations. They can be successful in professions related to drugs, pharmaceuticals or cosmetics, as their sensitive nature is often driven by their intuition.

They follow through on commitments and are often more committed than other people, which may cause them to be seen as shady by those around them. They are likely to succeed in a business environment that allows them to use their organizational skills.

They are unconventional individuals who are independent and do very well in upcoming careers such as television, aerospace or information technology.

They are extremely focused which gives them an advantage in achieving their goals. They tend to be happy, although they are susceptible to extreme mood swings. They can be successful in medicine, quality control or espionage roles.

They are sensitive and easily sense the emotions of others, although they may end up adopting those feelings for themselves. They easily care about and help others, so careers involving counseling, retail or even retailing are best. They can succeed in any field involving public service.

They tend to be the most sought after to carry out projects. They have a natural understanding that many people are not aware of as they do not boast. They are able to succeed in jobs such as mediation sales, teaching or even consulting.

These people always complete projects. They are extremely persuasive and can easily intimidate those who are not as confident. They tend to be solitary individuals with extraordinary organizational skills. They can be successful in positions such as agriculture, pensions and project management.

They are extremely systematic and prefer to work on their own. Even if they are part of teams, they will discover ways to work on their own. They can succeed in jobs that require intricate management.

These people are able to communicate easily with people of diverse backgrounds, have a cheerful disposition, and are extremely diplomatic. They can be successful in many fields, but are especially successful in jobs related to physical therapy, beauty or banking.

These people tend to go against the grain and have a very optimistic outlook. They are committed to changing the current system and can be successful in water-related jobs: fishing, boating, leisure industries.

Most of them are formed from life experiences and have a warm and welcoming disposition. They are able to quickly put themselves in the shoes of others and are successful in management or sales.

Chapter 7: Understanding The Fundamentals Of How The Science Of Numerology Operates.

The process of how numerology works is actually rather complex, and most of the time, a master numerologist is required to produce readings that are both thorough and accurate.

Even though you can quickly determine your life path number as well as numbers relating to things like your expression, personality, and soul urge by using fundamental calculations, the way in which these numbers interact with one another needs to be correctly interpreted in order to provide accurate results.

Numerology is based on the presumption that an individual's life and the universe as a whole are influenced by their birth date, their birth name, and a variety of other variables that surround them.

A numerology forecast can reveal extremely in-depth information when approached in this manner. As a result, it has the potential to offer sometimes astonishing insights about a person.

In the same way that some people look to horoscopes or astrology to interpret signs or destinies, some people believe that your name and birthday affect the journey that you will take and the characteristics that you have. It is believed that there are no coincidences in the universe and that your name and birthday affect who you are.

The Steps Involved In Performing A Numerology Reading

A reading in numerology requires a significant amount of mental arithmetic. These computations can continue into several layers of complexity, with individual numbers and number combinations conveying a variety of connotations.

Even the most fundamental reading based on your essential statistics may be quite illuminating.

On the other hand, in the same way that numbers are limitless, the numerology chart of a particular individual can continue to be interpreted from a variety of angles as an ongoing effort.

Both those who are just starting out and those who are looking for something more in-depth will find this to be an excellent introduction.

They begin with your name and date of birth and proceed to explain how your free numerology chart will not only tell you about yourself but also help to provide direction in your life and wellbeing by utilizing a combination of your life path number, birthday number, soul urge number, expression number, and personality number. This is done by starting with your life path number and working backwards.

The Life Path Number According to Numerology

Your life path number is considered to be the most significant number in Numerology. It is the cornerstone upon which the course of your life can be built.

In a same vein, it should represent who you are or who you aspire to be in terms of your personality and characteristics.

Your life path number can also provide insight into the chances and difficulties that lie ahead of you, as well as the life lessons that you are likely to pick up along the route.

There is a unique significance attached to each of the life path numbers.

To arrive to a conclusion, simply sum up all of the digits in your whole date of birth.

For instance, adding up April 4th, 1992 would result in the number 8. The year 1992 is represented by the equation $1 + 9 + 9 + 2$, which equals 21.

Now, put the two digits of 21 together, such as $2 + 1 = 3$, and get that number.

You should proceed in the same manner with all numbers that have two digits, continuing to add them up until you arrive at a number that only contains one digit.

For example, 19 may be written as $1 + 9 = 10$, followed by $1 + 0 = 1$. The final step in determining your life path number is to combine the 8 and the 3 together, which is 11.

Does it seem difficult? It's far simpler than you may imagine.

After you have established your life plan number, the next step is to look at what it has to say about you and your life in general. It is astounding how accurate a general understanding of the characteristics associated with one's life path number can be in describing an individual. Because of this, many people continue their quest to learn more about themselves by engaging in more in-depth reading.

The Number of Your Expression

An expression number is a personal number that is claimed to probe into your capabilities, ambitions, and personal objectives. This number is also sometimes referred to as your destiny number. It is also possible that it will bring to your attention any innate characteristics that you may possess.

Your expression number is determined by utilizing the Pythagorean method to translate the letters of your FULL birth name, including any middle names, into a numerical format.

In this particular kind of chart, a letter is matched up with a single-digit number. The grand total is then reduced to a single-digit figure at this point. Once more, the master numbers are applied to your destiny number, and they are not further decreased in any way.

Whichever expression number you are left with has a distinct meaning, and it works in combination with other core numbers to form a picture of who you are and what you're about as a person within the context of the larger universe.

Your Personal Soul Calling Number

In the field of numerology, your "Heart's Desire" number is also commonly referred to as your "Soul Urge" number. This might be interpreted as a reflection of your inner or more authentic self.

The most intriguing aspect of the soul desire number is the fact that it frequently discloses realities about individuals that those individuals only become aware of after a reading is over.

For instance, your heart's desire number may indicate that you secretly wish to have a position of authority. Or, that you are much more profound and need a higher degree of satisfaction in your life.

Alternately, you can have a requirement to have a sense of being respected or cared for... All of these characteristics frequently lie dormant under the surface, but when they are brought to light, they may be quite illuminating. Even if it means completely reorienting one's life on a different path in order to discover genuine pleasure.

The computation is comparable to others, with the exception that it uses your entire birth name. Having said that, you merely need to compute the value of the vowels in order to discover your inner needs or wants.

Your Personality Number According to Numerology

Only the consonants in your whole name are included in the calculation of your personality number, which is based on numerology.

After this, the same procedure of assigning a number to each letter is carried out before combining all of the numbers together and then reducing them to their component digits in order to arrive at a single-digit number or a master number.

Chapter 8: How To Calculate Your Life Path Number Or Destiny Number

What is the formula for determining your Numerology Life Path Number?

Analyzing the date you were born is the most straightforward method for getting started with dealing with numerology. In numerology, the goal is to discover the fundamental number behind everything. To do this, you need to eliminate digits until you get at a number with only one digit, omitting the digits 11 and 22, which are known as Master Numbers (more on this later). This single number is your very own personal Life Path Number.

Your Sun Sign in astrology is comparable to your Life Path Number in that it indicates aspects of your identity such as your strengths and weaknesses, your abilities and desires, and so on. Your Life Path Number reveals not only the flavor of your experiences but also the reasons behind why things have happened in the past, the present, and the future. To put it another way, it establishes an ordered and structured framework that sheds light on your previous life experiences.

Imagine that the 18th of August, 1989 is your birthday. In order to get your Life Path Number, you must first simplify this date by reducing each component to a single number, as follows:

The number of the month, 8, continues to be a single digit.

18 is simplified to 1 + 8 = 9, which equals the number 9.

The year 1989 may be rewritten as the sum of the digits 1, 9, 8, and 9. This comes out to 27. After that, 27 is reduced to 2 plus 7 which equals 9.

After then, we arrive at the number 26 by adding the shortened versions of the months, dates, and years (8 + 9 + 9). In the end, we add 2 and 6, which gives us 8. Your Life Path

Number is 8, and you and I both share the same birthday! If you were born on August 18, 1989, your Life Path Number is 8.

It is possible that at first it would appear frightening; however, once you see everything spelled out in this manner, it should become much less terrifying, right? Right!

In the study of numerology, what exactly are Master Numbers?

As was just explained, the only situation that you will not decrease the total amount is if you end up with either 11 or 22 points. These are known as Master Numbers, and they represent a heightened version of the root numbers that they are derived from (2 and 4, respectively). The Master Numbers point to a tremendous vibratory energy that is linked to learning, accomplishment, and success, but most typically in a situation that is more stressful or has higher stakes.

On June 18, 1942, for instance, Sir Paul McCartney was born, and he is often considered to be England's most famous Gemini. The total becomes 22 when this date is converted to its component parts (month = 6, day = 9, year = 7). Instead of simplifying this to a single digit, which would provide the number 4, the number 22 indicates the Master Number, which is the higher-octane iteration of the number 4, and it reveals McCartney's powerful "life goal."

In the practice of Numerology, how do you determine your Destination Number?

You may also utilize numerology to determine the root number of names or words. Our old friend Pythagoras can give some insight into this process. The following is a list of the particular numerical values that different letters are said to have according to his theories:

1 = A, J, S

2 = B, K, T

3 = C, L, U

4 = D, M, V

5 = E, N, W

6 = F, O, X

7 = G, P, Y

8 = H, Q, Z

9 = I, R

Numerologists refer to the root number linked with a person's name as their Destiny Number. Finding this number is simple when you use the technique described here. Calculating the root number of your entire name (first, middle, and last) is the first step towards discovering your Destiny Number. To do this, reduce each of your names to a single digit, and then add up the resulting numbers.

My Destiny Number, for instance, is 4, which is revealed by my whole name, which is ALIZA (1 + 3 + 9 + 8 + 1 = 22, which becomes 2 + 2 = 4). KELLY (2 + 5 + 3 + 3 7 = 20, which becomes 2 + 0 = 2) has a Destiny Number of 6 (since 4 + 2 = 7) as a result of the fact that 20 becomes 2 + 0 = 2.

While your Life Path will shed light on your overarching mission, your Destiny Number will provide insight into how you will put your overarching objectives into action. As a person with a Life Path 8, my objective in life is to develop abundance, and I will manifest this mission through the characteristics associated with my Destiny Number 6, which are nurturing, healing, and empathy. That is something that rings true!

Chapter 9: Everything You Need To Know About Numerology

You could have noticed that the number 4 tends to find its way to you in a fortunate way on a regular basis, or that you constantly come across the number 1 in its many forms across the globe. It is difficult to argue against the fact that numerical patterns often appear to us in a mysterious manner. Numerology is the study of occurrences exactly like this one.

Josh Siegel, a master numerologist who has been in practice for over two decades, argues that "Numerology is an old mystical science which attaches deeper meaning to numbers." "Numerology is an ancient mystical science which attributes deeper meaning to numbers," he says. "According to the concept that underpins it, everything, including people, exudes its own distinct vibration. Numerology in its modern form may be a strong self-help tool that can bring insight and direction when utilized appropriately.

According to Siegel, for instance, you can take your name and birth date and reduce them to a numeric code that will identify distinctive qualities and even the lessons you've learned in life. This is only one method among many others that you should keep in mind when you investigate your own crucial figures.

In this section, Siegel delves deeper into the fundamentals of numerology, exploring the many different kinds of numbers that may provide insightful information as well as the power and significance of each individual number.

How Numerology Came to Exist Siegel demonstrates that the philosophical underpinnings of numerology may be traced back thousands of years to the ancient civilizations of Egypt, Sumer, and India. He thinks that numbers have always been employed to depict the divine powers that operate in the natural world.

Pythagorus, a Greek philosopher and early mathematician who lived around 2500 BC and is credited with developing the Pythagorean Theorem that you learned in math class, taught that all things vibrate to their number and that even the planets resonate to their own frequency. Pythagorus's theory can be traced back to the Pythagorean Theorem. According to Siegel, the legend has it that Pythagoras visited Egypt and picked up some sacred wisdom while he was there. Traditions attribute to him some of the oldest sophisticated mathematics, geometry, and even the birth of western music, despite the fact that his life has become somewhat of a mythology.

How to Determine Your Numerology Life Path Number and What It Means

Locating your Life Path number is one of the first steps you can take in applying numerology to your own life. This number can provide insight into the areas of your life that require the most attention during your current incarnation. "It truly represents a problem you were born with that brings out attributes related with the number," argues Siegel. "It brings out qualities associated with the number."

If your Life Path number is 8, for instance, you may have issues with self-worth or empowerment, but you may also feel compelled to be a total boss in your work, whether that means competing for executive positions or creating your own firm. According to Siegel's explanation, "Over time, those on the 8 Life Route may learn to transcend their lessons and embrace the power that is implicit in their path number."

To put it another way, the purpose of this gathering is for us to reflect on the aspects of our Life Path number, incorporate those aspects into our job, and work toward bringing the more elevated aspects of that number into our everyday life. Siegel explains that, in a nutshell, it is an essential component of human progress.

How to Determine Your Personal Number for the Life Path

To determine your unique number for the Life Path:

1. First, sum the individual numbers for the month and the day that make up your birth date. After that, add the total for the year. For illustration's sake, a birth date of November 20th, 1985 would be computed as follows: 11 plus 20 equals 31 when added together as the month and day. Put the number 31 to the side.

2. Now, sum up all of the digits that make up the year that you were born. Continuing with the same illustration, 1 plus 9 plus 8 plus 5 equals 23.

3. The next step is to take the number for your birth year and add it to the number that was generated from your birth day as well as the month in which you were born. In this particular scenario, the answer is 54.

4. Next, combine the two numbers together to get a single new number. In this instance, 5 plus 4 equals 9, indicating the individual is on a Life Path number 9. Siegel argues that if you were to express it using more complex numerology, you would write it as 54/9.

What the Destiny Numbers, also known as the Natural Ability Numbers, Are and How They Are Calculated

To calculate your Destiny number, you may also utilize the information included on your birth certificate, which includes your entire name. Siegel believes that it's a bit of an outmoded word, due to the fact that the number you come up with doesn't always reflect your fate. Instead, it is illustrative of the natural abilities you possess. Siegel refers to it as the "Natural Ability" number for this particular reason.

Siegel adds that "it symbolizes capacities that are second nature, that you just know how to perform." "It represents capabilities that are second nature," To put it another way, it is not about anything you have to figure out or incorporate into your life, such as your Life Path number. You should consider working with both your Life Path number and your Natural Ability number in order to achieve the maximum success and sense of contentment.

Learn How to Calculate Your Destiny Number and Discover Your Natural Abilities Number \s1. First things first, keep in mind that a number corresponds to each and every letter in the alphabet. The answer to that question is as follows: A=1, B=2, C=3, D=4, E=5, F=6, G=7, H=8, I=9, J=1, K=2, L=3, M=4, N=5, O=6, P=7, Q=8, R=9, S=1, T=2, U=3, V=4, W=5, X=6, Y=7, Z=8.

2. You should provide your entire name when you are born now (first and last). Say it's SAMANTHA BELL. The resulting combination for the first name is 1 1 4 1 5281, while the result for the last name is 2533.

3. Add the letters of each name one by one, for example, Samantha equals 1+1+4+1+5+2+8+1, which equals 23. Bell is 2+5+3+3 = 13.

4. Finally, sum up the totals, which should equal 36 (23 + 13).

5. To produce a new number, add the two numbers together as shown in step five. Samantha has a Natural Ability (or Destiny) number of 9, which can be derived by adding 3 and 6, which equals 9. Siegel points out that it may alternatively be written as 36/9.

Master Numbers, Defined

Numerologists refer to the rare double-digit numbers that they will not reduce to a single digit as "Master Numbers." These numbers are not reducible to a single digit. According to Siegel's explanation, these exceptional numbers bring the potential for tremendous reward but also provide challenges to the individuals whose numerology charts include them.